Understanding Teacher Stress
In Light of Educational Reform

A Theoretical & Practical Approach
Andrea Thompson, Ph.D.

authorHOUSE™

1663 LIBERTY DRIVE, SUITE 200
BLOOMINGTON, INDIANA 47403
(800) 839-8640
WWW.AUTHORHOUSE.COM

© 2005 Andrea Thompson, Ph.D. All Rights Reserved.

No part of this book may be reproduced, stored in a retrieval system, or transmitted by any means without the written permission of the author.

First published by AuthorHouse 11/28/05

ISBN: 1-4208-9122-7 (sc)
ISBN: 1-4208-9121-9 (dj)

Printed in the United States of America
Bloomington, Indiana

This book is printed on acid-free paper.

Contents

Preface vii

Section One 1
- Educational Reform: Maintaining Continuity
- Scrutiny and Adequate Yearly Progress
- Retaining Our Most Vital Resource: Teachers
- Anxiety-producing situations & propensity for using inappropriate coping strategies

Section Two 15
- Impact of Increased Accountability: Principal's Perspective
- Why Examine Teacher Stress?
- Understanding Stress
- Stress: Evaluative Beliefs
- Stress: Predictability and Controllability
- Stress: Demands and Consequences

Section Three 29
- Stress: Self-efficacy and Coping Abilities
- Coping: Primary or Secondary Appraisal
- Coping: Emotion-focused or Problem-focused
- Coping: A Theoretical Examination of Techniques Used
- Actual problem solving takes place in several ways: Transfer-of-training and writing

Section Four 41
- Stress Management Programs for Educators: A Necessity
- Stress Management Programs: Goals, Approaches, and Design
- Stress Management Interventions: Three Levels
- Leadership-Participation:
- **Stress Management Program Design**: Concerns and Focus
- Evaluation of Stress Management Programs

Conclusion 61

Preface

This four-section book examines the underlying theories of teacher stress within the context of educational reform, and in so doing focuses on elements which influence the change process, and variables which are likely to emerge. Understanding Teacher Stress contributes to the body of knowledge concerning teacher stress, and creates an awareness of theoretical underpinnings of stress management program design. It also provides practical information on ways in which stress management can be used to modify and eliminate teacher stress. It is the writer's belief that knowledge of factors and consequences underlying stress will bear implications on teacher education college curriculums, educational leadership, policy making, and educational practices. The first section explores the immense undertaking of maintaining continuity in light of educational reform. Mention is made of the No Child Left Behind Act 2001 required evidence of adequate yearly progress (AYP), and teachers' response to public scrutiny of published state assessment results. This section also addresses the importance of retaining teachers, the most

Understanding Teacher Stress

vital resource in the change process, paying close attention to their coping strategies as they seek to meet accountability demands. Section two presents research supporting the impact of increased accountability on principals and teachers, and examines the necessity for exploring and understanding teacher stress. It further mentions the impact that evaluative beliefs, predictability, and controllability have on teacher stress. The section ends with a detailed theoretical explanation of how demands and consequences affect teacher stress, and ultimately teacher efficacy. Section three focuses on coping strategies by first guiding readers through a theoretical examination of appraisal methods, and emotion or problem-focused approaches used. Section four details the desired goals, approaches, and designs used in stress management programs, while focusing on various levels of stress management interventions. Finally, an empirical and non-empirical journey is taken into findings of various stress management programs being used in the field.

SECTION ONE

Educational Reform: Maintaining Continuity

All organizations experience a growth process (Beatty & Ulrich, 1991), a move from one stage of maturity to another; a move characterized as change. The public school system, being no different from other organizations, experiences change within the context of educational reform. The change may be evolutionary or revolutionary, crisis-triggered or planned, and in some cases incremental. Freeman and Cameron (1993) purports that in some instances change may be convergent in nature in which no structural uprooting takes place instead the same things are being accomplished in a different way. The recent No Child Left Behind Act, 2001, is by no means convergent. It represents far-reaching transformations in terms of accountability, curriculum, teacher quality, and parental involvement.

Implementation of such massive restructuring, challenges educational leaders with the monumental task of balancing continuity and high performance with change, all the while being aware that change disturbs complacency and stability thereby inciting issue tension (Leanna & Barry, 2000). Issue tensions are incited mainly because change comes with benefits and adversities as it redirects, amends, tweaks, modifies, and regulates. Whether a leader's manner in bringing about change is punctuated (Romanelli & Tushman, 1994) or revolutionary in its approach, it disturbs the inertia and will not detract from the predictable tension.

A belief in the change/reform is vital to it's success therefore educational leaders have the immense undertaking of convincing teachers that the reform is similar to their pedagogical belief, and will not place them in a position of professional compromise (Moriarty, Edmonds, Blatchford, & Martin, 2001). Such feelings of compromise only serve to incite job dissatisfaction, a variable found to be positively correlated with role stress (Van Sell, Brief, & Schuler, 1997) but not surprising, as it is expected that roles will increase and transform as organizational changes are implemented (Kahn, Wolfe, Quinn, Snoek, & Rosenthal, 1964).

It's important to note that educational reform movements are ongoing irrespective of America's concern with teacher retention, burnout, and attrition. It leads us then to wonder, how effective will these changes be if the afore-mentioned issues are not addressed? As school leaders lead reform initiatives such as the No Child Left Behind Act (NCLB), they must be cognizant of elements that create resistance to change, and emerging or emanating variables that are likely to result during the change process.

Concern with resistance to change means that leaders will focus on:
1) Teachers' readiness for change;
2) Acknowledgement of discrepancies rendering a need for change
3) Teachers' belief that they are able to carry out the desired change (Armenakasis, Harris, & Mossholder, 2000) leading to a question of self-efficacy.

Concern with emerging and emanating variables that are likely to result in the change process means that leaders will focus on:
1) Teachers' stress level during change
2) Coping abilities
3) Teacher-efficacy which ultimately impacts students' self-efficacy

Given Bandura's (1997) theory that, "self-efficacy is an individual's conviction that he or she can successfully execute the behavior necessary to produce a desired outcome" (p. 450), it is essential that educational leaders encourage and promote an environment in which teachers *believe that they are capable of executing change.* When change is associated with high stakes accountability, an important factor to consider is teachers' possible anger towards low-performing students. Interestingly, research indicates that teacher efficacy has a lot to do with the propensity for such behavior, as is evidenced in Gordon's (2001) study of a group of high efficacy teachers in comparison to low efficacy elementary teachers, in which the high efficacy group reported high self-confidence, and was less likely to feel anger towards low performing and disruptive students. On the other hand, the low efficacy group had less confidence in the ability to manage students and was more prone to anger and stress.

As educational leaders seek to incorporate change in keeping with high student achievement, the knowledge that efficacy and stress correlate, leads to a new focus: *increasing teacher efficacy and reducing stress*. *Understanding Teacher Stress* is designed to open dialogue on variables which are likely to impact teachers' ability to perform effectively in the face of change, but specifically to examine stress coping strategies and effective stress management interventions.

Scrutiny and Adequate Yearly Progress

Assessment of past educational reforms disclose that quality of instruction was and still is a main focus (Chance, 1992) therefore it comes as no surprise that since teachers are responsible for instructional delivery, when accountability indicates that learning did not occur, teachers are often subject to public scrutiny and criticism (Dunham, 1992). For many teachers this is disheartening. Researchers have indicated that when teachers are pounded by scrutiny and criticism they are made to feel as though they are the problem (Boyer, 1988). This further incites feelings of isolation and stress (Cox & Wood, 1980). The high accountability aspect of the No Child Left Behind Act, 2001, does not serve to alleviate this public scrutiny in light of the fact that annual report cards detailing student achievement is made public, and scrutiny and criticism are now linked to consequences. Let's examine a common perception of public scrutiny and arrive at ways in which the perception can be changed. A school that is labeled as *not* having met Adequate Yearly Progress (AYP) is immediately placed under prescription. Some teachers are likely to perceive this as an embarrassment. The school's staff, administrators, and teachers, now have two choices:

1.) Continue utilizing the same instructional strategies and focus, and stand the chance of arriving at the same results; or
2.) View the result as a diagnosis and opportunity to target and address problem areas by incorporating research-based strategies, and raising teacher and student efficacy.

It is recommended that educational leaders take responsibility for leading and modeling the change in perception, and inspiring the faculty to move full force ahead in spite of the previous year's accountability report. This is not a time to 'lick wounds." It is time to lead the dream and vision. Taking a line from the old adage "if you fall out of the race it's no disgrace, just pick yourself from off the ground." Picking yourself up begins with the first faculty meeting after a summer break. It is the beginning of a new school year, a fresh start, an ideal time to set the tone and change perceptions. This is when school leaders will spend 20% of pre-planning mentioning past failures and indicating areas slated for improvement, 30% explaining plans for implementing new solutions, strategies, and teacher support; and 50% of the time raising teacher efficacy.

In a recent interview of teachers who were returning to a school which had *not* met adequate yearly progress, 15 of the 28 teachers indicated that they were too embarrassed to face parents on the first day of school. They felt as though they had failed the children and the community. The remaining teachers expressed anger and refused to accept any responsibility for student failure. They indicated that they had tried their best but that due to lack of parental support, students were unable to rise to their full potential. Evidently, there is a lack of belief in students' ability to achieve in spite of their home situation. It is for these reasons that 50% of pre-planning is allotted to raising teacher efficacy. The new school year should not begin with teachers nursing feelings of anger towards low performing students; and others moping about past failures. An atmosphere of assertiveness needs to reign. One in which everyone is prepared to work collaboratively, tackling the weakest areas. Learning new strategies and solutions is the easy task. Teachers' attitude towards implementing new strategies and solutions is where the emphasis is most needed.

Without teachers, strategies, and solutions cannot be implemented. Theories may be found but operationalizing theories, concepts, and strategies is what teachers do best. It means therefore that we must move our teachers beyond the point of being crippled by sensitivity to public scrutiny and criticism, and instead, lead them in the direction of utilizing data analysis results and evaluations as diagnostic and prescriptive tools in pursuit of student achievement. Fortunately for the educational organization, teachers are buoyant beings, who are quick to recover from negativities. Those who venture into teaching, do so knowing that they will never become wealthy therefore it must only be for a love of seeing others learn, develop, and grow why teachers remain in the profession. Teachers work above and beyond the call of duty. The ringing of the school bell only means that we are sending home our precious 'charges' it never means that the task of planning for their learning is over. Long after everyone's' work is done teachers can be found planning for the next day's lessons and seeking resources which will support lessons, and seal concepts and skills.

During summer months, weekends, and holiday breaks, teachers can be found in stores and way-out places scavenging for artifacts and resources which support real-life learning. This is all for the sake of enhancing student achievement. Teachers can be seen during the late hours of night, grading papers and scribbling feedbacks which serve to help and guide students. They sacrifice their own self-interest for the good of their students; purchasing classroom materials from personal funds; remaining after school to meet with parents and to assist students who may need that extra help; participating in literacy, technology, and math nights, and extra programs which serve to aid students and parents. In addition to all the above, teachers must find time to continually stay abreast of 'best practices' in an effort to improve their ability to effectively deliver differentiated and technology-enhanced instructions. Teachers are aware that interest in children goes beyond delivering instructions, and all they ask for are supplies and support as they listen to their students' ideas and opinions, and gently correct misconceptions while valuing them. A teacher's role is all-inclusive and impacts the whole child. Bearing this in mind, it means that we must seek ways to retain our teachers and ensure that they are able to function at full capacity; not laden with stress and other issues. It is therefore vital that educational leaders' develop the ability to recognize *teacher stress* and direct teachers towards effective intervention strategies.

Retaining Our Most Vital Resource: Teachers

At a time when failure to meet accountability is laden with scrutiny and consequences, our school systems will need hardy and organizationally-committed teachers who use effective stress coping strategies, and maintain high self-efficacy. It means then that teachers who do not naturally possess these attributes must be nurtured and encouraged through intervention programs. The hardy teacher by nature exhibits control, commitment, and acceptance of challenges (Maddi, 2002). In a situation where a school fails to meet adequate yearly progress, the hardy teacher, instead of feeling threatened by the impending consequences, is instead ready to rise to the challenge of meeting the goals of accountability and student achievement, and is in control of the energy and strategy needed to tread the path. Further, hardy teachers take a problem-focused rather than an emotion-focused approach to coping with stress (Kobasa & Puccetti, 1983). Realistically, not all teachers have the ability to cope with stress therefore there is a necessity for stress management intervention programs in the educational organization.

All educational leaders are desirous of having a highly committed faculty, mainly because these highly committed individuals are often characterized as exhibiting:
  a) A strong desire to maintain membership within the organization
  b) Acceptance and adherence to the values and goals of the organization
  c) A willingness to work towards accomplishing the goals of the organization (Porter, Steers, Mowday, & Boulian, 1974).

Such levels of commitment are ideal in a school setting, especially one that is faced with trying to rebound from failing to meet adequate yearly progress. The writer posits that if educational leaders maintain a climate of positive belief, and high expectancy that all teachers are in fact hardy and committed to meeting the goals of accountability, then teachers are likely to respond accordingly. This is then likely to create a trickling-effect wherein, teachers' belief and expectancy of students' ability to raise their achievement level is likely to create the desired result. The expectancy is that teachers will behave in a manner that is expected of them.

In the event that hardiness and commitment is lacking, and instead, teachers exhibit signs of stress, it is wise to observe closely, actions which individuals are likely to engage in as stress coping mechanisms (Kyriacou & Sutcliffe, 1978). Several such actions are frequent absenteeism and tardiness (Hanisch, 2000; Ones, 2002). Meeting adequate yearly progress requires that teachers are consistently on task, and ready to meet the daily challenges of educating students therefore, absenteeism as a form of coping is highly unacceptable. Frequent absenteeism interrupts the flow of instruction (Bruno, 2002). In fact, because these behaviors interrupt a school's effectiveness and research has linked increased absenteeism (Maturi, 1992) to *teacher stress*, it is important to make provisions for intervention. Stability must be maintained so that student-learning is uninterrupted, and teachers learn coping strategies to assist them in dealing with situations which are likely to arise and impact what they do best; educate.

Anxiety-producing situations & propensity for using inappropriate coping strategies

During a middle school pre-planning meeting, 37 teachers were asked to describe their reaction to the principals 'call to action' for the upcoming school year. Twenty-two teachers explained that while listening to all that was required of them for the upcoming school year, they began experiencing an overwhelming sense of role overload, while 17 teachers sensed a tremendous demand of their time. All 37 teachers jokingly mentioned that as a relief, their sick and personal days would be fully utilized during the upcoming year. When asked what aspect of the presentation triggered such feelings, all teachers mentioned:

1) Overloaded classes, rendering an unrealistic amount of students to be effectively served by one teacher.
2) Additional duties outside of instruction.

Although the principal mentioned that teachers who participated in extra duties would be compensated, this did not seem to reduce feelings of work and role overload. Teachers were still not overjoyed at taking on additional responsibilities. Educational leaders must be realistic about the demands being placed on teachers and must ensure that they are aware of the support and resources that are in place to assist them in meeting these demands. This is the first step to averting teachers' propensity to relieve the pressures of role overload or work increase by resorting to frequent tardiness and absences.

Another anxiety-producing factor which detracts from meeting reform goals is some teachers' inability to foster and maintain a healthy working relationship with their colleagues. In a recent dialogue with two teachers, Ms Green and Mr. Ennis, it was noted that both teachers reported feelings of stress and used tardiness as a means of avoiding co-teaching. Neither teacher wanted to co-teach because for years they had both worked in isolation. Interestingly, both teachers were great at advising other teachers. They had amassed years of experience and were valuable resources to the younger staff. Unfortunately, now that they had to collaboratively teach, each felt that one was trying to outshine the other. Needless to say, while these teachers bickered daily, students were the ones being short-changed and the goals of educational reform were being neglected.

Mr. Ennis, a fully certified teacher, complained that he felt like an aide mainly because Ms Green confined him to one section of the room, refused to jointly plan and deliver lessons, and regularly required that he hand out worksheets or sit with disruptive children. Students in the class were frequently told *not to bother Mr. Ennis with questions rather all questions should be directed to the classroom teacher.* This was Ms Green's subtle way of establishing boundaries. Verbal confrontations between both teachers increased, and each began complaining of being *stressed*. Fortunately, the assistant principal was able to recognize signs of stress in addition to the fact that both teachers were frequently and increasingly tardy as a means of avoiding each other. He realized that they were both uneasy with co-teaching, and both felt scrutinized by the other. They were immediately scheduled to attend co-teaching workshops in which they learned how to develop interpersonal communication skills, and to collaboratively plan. As both teachers armed themselves with new knowledge and became refocused, there was an improvement in their working relationship and a reduction in tardiness. The goals of educational reform were again on track and counter productive coping behaviors ceased.

Unfortunately however, the outcome was not as great for Mr. Williams and Ms Rothberg, who used several forms of counter productive coping mechanisms as a means of expressing what they considered to be the principal's disregard of their roles as music and physical education teachers. Having failed to meet the previous year's adequate yearly progress, the principal decided to increase reading class time by narrowing the curriculum. Class periods for physical education and music were significantly reduced while reading and math periods increased. Students whose reading and math scores were low, lost elective classes and in turn were required to attended remedial reading and math classes. The music and physical education teachers were angry. They met with the principal and in no uncertain terms informed him that he had no regard for any subject area that was not considered a core subject. He responded by informing them that his focus concerns only subject areas on which students would be tested. He further indicated that it was more important that the test scores reflect that students were functioning at a proficient level in math and reading, and not how fast they could run or how well they could sing. This infuriated the teachers who became more frustrated with trying to change the principal's perspective.

Both teachers eventually decided that since the principal did not value their subject area, then their tardiness and absences would go unnoticed. Realizing that core teachers' relied on music and physical education periods as their preparation time, Mr. Williams and Ms Rothberg began arriving tardy on many days, and did not seem to care that it would be documented. As far as they were concerned, the principal did not value their roles, and neither would the teachers. Between them they had enough sick days accrued to make an impact, and so the excessive absences and tardiness began. Before the school year ended they applied for transfers to other school. In this instance, the principal's actions were driven by his concern with public scrutiny and accountability. The school was being scrutinized based on the results of students' achievement in math and reading; and meeting accountability in these areas became more important than retaining a music and physical education teacher. When asked what his feelings were regarding the recent turnover, his response was that unless it was a core teacher then it really didn't matter.

SECTION TWO

Impact of Increased Accountability: Principal's Perspective

During a time when principals are likely to be labeled *low-performing or high-performing* based on their school's performance on state assessment exams, no doubt they will resort to creative means of assuring that their schools do meet accountability demands. It is unfortunate but research indicates that narrowing of curriculum, teaching to the test, and in some cases elimination of recess in lieu of increased instructional time are some of those creative methods. While some may criticize these moves as being insensitive, others may praise these leaders as doing whatever it takes to ensure that student achievement soars.

Research indicates that principals complain of *increased pressure and workload* as the need to meet accountability increases. Needless to say, the possibility that this is likely to occur is not encouraging to those who aspire to be principals mainly because *increased workload* is viewed as a heightening of principals' managerial and instructional leadership roles (Cooley & Shen, 2003). It was further supported by Ryan's (2001) report that principals regarded *increased workload* as being a major stressor. Additionally, Howley and Pendarvis (2002) reported that school districts are experiencing difficulty recruiting and retaining principals, largely due to complaints of *job pressure* resulting from increased accountability demands. Likewise, Cusick (2003) also found that the already growing principal shortage is escalating because accountability-based consequences require the removal of principals in failing schools. Armed with this knowledge, prospective principal-applicants are less inclined to apply.

Added to job pressure and increased workload is another variable; *job insecurity*. Spitulnik, (2001), found that when principals were faced with elimination of tenure prompted by educational reform, they experienced *job insecurity* which served to incite feelings of stress. In Schulte's (2000) study, while principals reported an appreciation for the increase in instructional focus and improved teaching strategy, resulting from the demands of increased accountability, they stated that it also inflicted too much pressure on both administrators and teachers. Considering that increased accountability does have positive effects on instructional delivery, it is safe to say that along with the increased demands, focus should be placed on assisting administrators in dealing with increased *job pressures, work overload increase, and job insecurity;* variables that take away from the positives. The fact that principals view these variables as stressors means that policy makers need to include an added feature to increased accountability; stress management intervention. Flynn (2000) supports the need for this type of intervention, based on the finding that stress can cause principal burnout. A burnt-out principal does not support the goals of educational reform. Further, it was found that younger principals and those with less experience reported a greater level of stress, and principals with larger schools exhibited a higher level of exhaustion. This speaks to the need for stress management intervention which will assist principals in utilizing coping strategies.

In spite of increased job pressure, principals are resolute about minimizing low performance and ineffectiveness in an effort to avert the consequences associated with high stakes accountability. Their actions are supported by research which shows that an organization's success is dependent on employees' level of performance (Campbell, 1990). It means therefore that significant teacher performance is vital to student achievement. The goals of the NCLB Act, 2001 cannot be achieved if there is a gap between goal achievement and educators' ability to perform. It is therefore not amazing to find that principals will not hesitate to dismiss under-performing teachers. Having to do so however takes its toll. Results of a study examining the impact of teacher termination on elementary school principals (Heiser, 2001) revealed that more experienced principals were concerned with the extra effort required to assist and support ineffective teachers, while less-experienced principals struggled with the impact that termination would have on teachers. It means that having to deal with ineffective and under-performing teachers in a time of high stakes accountability is an issue for all principals. Clearly some do not want to expend the energy and time necessary to guide and mentor teachers into becoming high-performing employees.

One principal stated that his focus was *hiring high-performing teachers* to ensure that his school met adequate yearly progress. His exact words were, "I don't have time to baby-sit." Needless to say, for low-performing teachers, the *threat of termination* and *impending job loss* is enough to compound their dilemma mainly because in addition to feelings of *job-insecurity*, it also triggers *poor self-efficacy* (Bandura, 1988). Given that studies indicate that teacher efficacy influences student outcomes (Ross, 1992), and teachers with high self-efficacy are prone to try innovative means towards helping students learn (Stein & Wang, 1988; Allinder, 1994), it is wise to invest in assisting low performing teachers and ensuring that teachers' self-efficacy remain intact. Again, if the ultimate focus is raising student achievement and meeting adequate yearly progress, by all means, time invested in ensuring that our teachers are competent and able, is time well spent. Who, if not teachers, will guide our students towards optimal achievement?

Why Examine Teacher Stress?

Reports detailing the effects of accountability, sanctions, and consequences are well documented. Turchi, Johnson, Owens, and Montgomery (2002) presented findings in which teachers in low performing schools complained of experiencing *job insecurity*, and were inclined to feel as though they were being assessed rather than supported. Considering that sanctions for repeated low performance necessitates changing staff and revamping curriculum, *job threat* or feelings of *job insecurity* is realistic for everyone involved. Teachers experience job threat when they are unable to meet the job's demands that are perceived as being difficult and unattainable (Kyriacou, 1987). At this point, educators may need to reach out and inspire each other. In so doing, convey the assurance that the task at hand is indeed attainable. Remind each other that support is available in the form of professional development, stress coping strategies workshops, and any other district supported intervention. When teachers are faced with job threat and job insecurity, they believe that they are incapable of coping (Bandura, 1988) but lack of belief in the ability to cope is not the only repercussion of job insecurity. Lim (1997) theorized that job insecurity is detrimental to an individual's job attitude and behavior; two factors which are counterproductive to high performance.

At a time when it is imperative that schools must show adequate yearly progress or deal with consequences set forth, the probability that teachers are likely to leave the profession due to job stress makes it necessary to research and find means of alleviating the conditions therewith. Policy makers, principals, and parents need every teacher functioning at their highest potential. In addition, the knowledge that stress is inevitable during change because change incites feelings of susceptibility and insecurities about expanded roles (Nelson, Cooper, & Jackson, 1995) is even more justification for examining teacher stress. It is well to note also that throughout our dialogue, *job pressure, increased workload, job-insecurity, job threat, and teacher efficacy* were deemed to be stressors, which greatly impacted both principals and teachers. Given that these issues are counterproductive to educational policies' intent, it means therefore, that in the interests of achieving educational reform goals, policy makers need to ensure that educators, who are at the frontline of implementation, understand the nature of stress; examine stress coping abilities proven to be effective; and are able to determine the effectiveness of available stress intervention program and strategies. We begin by first defining stress.

Understanding Stress

A major part of understanding stress is to first develop the ability to recognize and define it. Stress can be manifested and defined from a physiological, psychological, or transactional standpoint. Seyle (1975) perceived stress as a physiological reaction in which the body responds to demands in a process called General Adaptive Syndrome (GAS) constituting *alarm, resistance*, and finally *exhaustion*. At the alarm stage, the body's reaction to stressful conditions trigger the secretion of chemicals, which cause anxiety-producing conditions ultimately stressing the body. In an attempt to defy stress, the body may opt to adjust to the stressor; this is regarded as the resistance phase. As the stressor or stressful situation continues, eventually the body's ability to adjust is minimized and fatigue sets in. This is described as the exhaustion stage, which eventually causes the body to return to the initial alarm phase.

Understanding Teacher Stress

Envision a principal announcing and discussing an upcoming instructional assessment or observation. Teachers' reactions and responses will differ. For teachers who resent the very thought of being scrutinized, instructional audits unnerve and distresses them, eventually creating a physical reaction in which the body enters into an alarm phase rendering anxiety-producing reactions. In an attempt to defy stress, the body then ventures into a resistance phase in which it tries to adjust to the thought of being scrutinized. As the principal continues to explain in detail the instructional auditing or observation process, the body's inability to adjust to the very thought of being scrutinized may produce fatigue and exhaustion; hence an ongoing feeling of stress which may not be alleviated until the instructional auditing process ends.

Remaining in this stressful mode until the audit is completed may affect a teacher's ability to effectively perform. One can only imagine the physical reactions that are likely to occur as these teachers await the results of state assessments. There are principals who avoid teachers who frequently react to challenges in this manner; instead they fortify themselves with teachers who enjoy rising to a challenge. There are also teachers who welcome showcasing their instructional prowess and whole-heartedly welcome scrutiny of their performance. These teachers may experience a different type of stress called eustress. Seyle (1975) identified two types of stresses: *eustress* and *distress*. Eustress, considered good stress, is the type sought out by individuals who enjoy challenging situations and do not perceive those situations as being distressful. Distress however is viewed as bad stress, the type that creates feelings of anguish. It's wise to acknowledge that many teachers may experience the alarm stage but are capable of overcoming these feelings of despair at the resistance stage. It's no wonder then that many teachers are able to function so well in spite of anguishing feelings.

Stress: Evaluative Beliefs

Research shows that people's evaluative beliefs influence their perception of events as either eustress or distress, and that stressors remain neutral until individuals impose their appraisal or evaluation upon them (Woolfolk & Richardson, 1978). As teachers become aware of impending scrutiny in the form of assessments, observations, or instructional audits, their discernment and understanding of the implications of these measures are factored. If a teacher's evaluative belief is that instructional audit is indeed negative scrutiny or 'witch hunting', it immediately triggers distress. The same can be said for a school's test results being made public. If teacher's evaluative beliefs label this sort of scrutiny in a negative light, then no doubt it will generate distress. The fact that consequences are associated with poor assessment results is one factor that is likely to drive teachers' evaluative beliefs of the process towards a negative response. Considering the reality of these consequences, it is realistic that some teachers may worry that if instructional audits do not yield positive results then their job is threatened. To complicate matters, a teacher's ability to cope is factored, considering that the inability to cope with perceived threatening situations is also defined as stress (Seaward, 1997).

On a lighter note, consider teachers who welcome assessments and accountability, believing that knowledge of these results can be beneficial in several ways, and that if their students did well, then it means that instructional strategies used were effective and now failing schools can employ similar strategies. These teachers may also believe that knowledge of how poorly their students are doing is a chance to confront target areas that will need focus, and in turn give students the help they really need. In a recent interview of 15 teachers who taught at a school which regularly met its AYP, teachers expressed feelings of nervousness and anticipation each year as they await the results. They all described feelings of anxiety based on fear of the consequences set forth. Fourteen teachers mentioned feeling pressured at maintaining the momentum but they delighted in the challenge of preparing students for high achievement, and they believed in assessment as a way of measuring student achievement. This is an example of *eustress*. Here teachers enjoy rising to the challenge. The writer posits that as teachers develop an awareness of *eustress* and *distress*, finally understanding the benefits, detriment, and impact that evaluative beliefs have on both, there is a possibility that they will function within a climate of *eustress*.

Stress: Predictability and Controllability

Possner and Leitner (1981) introduced predictability and controllability as two means of determining whether a situation evoked *eustress* or *distress*. When a stressor is *predictable* it allows individuals an opportunity to make preparations, in which case, the situation or stressor is likely to elicit *eustress*. If a stressor is *unpredictable*, then it is likely to trigger *distress*. The fact that the principal gave ample notice that instructional audit would be forthcoming means that predictability allowed teachers ample time to employ safety nets, and *control* the outcome through preparation. If instructional audits were unannounced, it would be more likely to elicit distress, although it can be said that if teachers are consistently on task then an unannounced audit should not create distress. It all points to the fact that some teachers regard scrutiny as being stressful. The same can be said for state assessment exams, teachers are able to use predictability and ample preparation time to influence the outcome. Teachers are aware that students are required to take state assessment exams, and that these results will determine whether the school shows adequate yearly progress. This points to predictability but on the other hand, teachers do not have control over the consequences associated with unmet adequate yearly progress, and this may be the troubling area.

The fact that reform mandates are top-led does not mean that teachers do not have control. Teachers work in isolation and their classrooms are little businesses in which every teacher is a CEO, which provides controllability. The school system provides resources and keeps teachers abreast of best practices and research-based strategies. Teachers then implement these techniques and practices. How effective implementation of these techniques and strategies are, will reflect on state assessments results.

The theory of predictability and controllability also bears implications for staff development timing, and most importantly the first few days of school opening. This is a time when educational leaders are able to convey their expectations, inform teachers of the availability of resources, present workshops supporting the required tasks, influence perceptions, correct misconceptions, and most importantly provide time for preparation. Sporadically informing teachers of their requirements throughout the school year, instead of doing so from the onset, sets the stage for distress based on unpredictability and inadequate preparation time.

Stress: Demands and Consequences

From a psychological standpoint, McGrath ((1976) viewed stress as a process in which individuals perceive themselves as being *incapable of responding to demands which are laden with consequences*. This points to self-efficacy and continued focus on the consequences associated with the stressor. When a person perceives an inability to meet the demands required of the perceived stressor, awareness of the inability becomes stressful. Consider teachers who focus mainly on the consequences associated with failing to meet accountability demands. How does this focus impact teacher performance? Is this focus likely to serve as a driving force, enthusing and motivating teachers to work really hard so as to avoid these consequences? If so, then the type of stress evoked may be considered *eustress*. Alternatively, will focus on consequences dishearten and demotivate teachers to the point where they are unable to encourage students to rise to the challenge? If so, it is time to assess teacher efficacy, evaluative beliefs, stress coping abilities, and guide teachers towards a change in perception. This is especially necessary in light of the fact that there is no indication that these consequences are being eliminated.

Teachers need to believe that they are capable of raising student achievement. It begins with their belief that each child is capable of achieving. In Greenwood, Olejnik, & Parkay's (1990) study, belief patterns were found to be significantly related to stress. (A scary notion indeed, especially when research shows that evaluative beliefs influence our labeling of situations as eustress or distress). Sixty-five percent of the teachers studied, believed that all teachers were generally capable of motivating students to achieve, interestingly however, only 85% believed that *they* were individually capable of motivating students towards high academic achievement. Fortunately, teachers who exhibited positive belief patterns experienced less stress than their counterparts. This result bears implications for stress management programs that focus on changing perceptions and belief patterns. The writer posits that a well-constructed stress management program is capable of providing teachers with the necessary skills to improve coping strategies, raise self-efficacy, and influence a positive and rational belief system.

A *transactional approach* to defining stress may also assist us in understanding teacher stress. Lazarus and Folkman (1984) viewed stress as a transactional relationship between individuals and the environment, which is appraised as being exhausting, strenuous, and more demanding than available resources. Do our teachers view their work environment as being strenuous, and if so, why? Educational leaders can combat this problem by meeting with teachers to hear their concerns and reasons for appraising their environment as being exhausting and strenuous, and what available resources they deem as being inadequate. Addressing this at the building level ultimately clears the way for instructional focus. In the past, teachers have cited issues such as school building's poor physical condition, lack of teaching resources, and lack of adequate training. If teachers do not estimate an environment as being burdensome and exhausting, and instead perceive that available resources are sufficient in meeting the goals of educational reform, stressful feelings will likely decrease. Teachers concerns usually entail supplies and support.

SECTION THREE

Stress: Self-efficacy and Coping Abilities

An examination of the definitions of stress points to *perceptions* and *beliefs*, which ultimately points to *self-efficacy*. In addition, *perceived inability* to cope with stressful events (Cencirulo, 2001) also points to a lack of self-efficacy. How do we begin addressing this issue? Research shows that teachers must first learn stress coping abilities, which is shown to relate to self-efficacy. An investigation of the relationship between stress, anxiety and self-efficacy for 149 urban elementary teachers (Ealy, 1993) found that higher levels of self-efficacy were linked to lower levels of anxiety. In support, Slack-William's (1996) findings in which the relationship between self-efficacy, and state/trait anxiety with teachers' coping abilities was examined, indicating that the relationship between self-efficacy and anxiety was based on teachers' personal coping ability. Teachers who used coping strategies successfully reduced anxiety more than teachers who did not use coping strategies. Both researchers (Ealy, 1993; Slack-William, 1996) also found that teachers with more experience had lower levels of anxiety. The writer proposes that the extent to which educators are capable of coping with work-related stress *will* impact their ability to pursue and reach intended goals; hence the need for an examination of stress-coping abilities.

Coping: Primary or Secondary Appraisal

Research indicates that the first step in coping is to appraise the perceived stressful event or situation using a primary or secondary appraisal method (Lazarus & Folkman, 1984). *Primary appraisal* entails assessing the situation in relation to a person's well being. Teachers who choose to use a primary appraisal process would assess the impact of educational reform, on their well-being. A prime example is a teacher who is not willing to exert the energy required to implement changes, or may find this exertion as being too stressful. During this process, situations or events are viewed as immaterial, stressful, detrimental, intimidating, or taxing. Questions likely to surface are, can this stressor create a harmful impact, loss, or threat? In view of the consequences associated with the failure to meet accountability demands, some teachers may perceive *harmful impact* as being *job threat* in the event failure occurs. Once these questions are answered and it is determined that the stressor is damaging or non-beneficial, the individual will try to perceive it differently or employ behavioral strategies to accommodate coping. Perceived self-efficacy is a vital component at this point because if the individual believes that the ability to change the situation exists, a new behavior will reflect that perception.

A *secondary appraisal* method involves *focusing on solutions* for coping with the situation. Teachers who choose to use a secondary appraisal approach are more concerned with the *availability of resources to handle the stressor*, in which case, instead of worrying about how they would be viewed during public scrutiny of assessment scores, they are more concerned with acquiring the resources needed to meet accountability demands or educational reform. Considering the benefits likely to be derived from this way of appraising demands, an investment in intervention strategies which are likely to guide teachers in using appropriate and effective appraisal methods would be highly beneficial.

Coping: Emotion-focused or Problem-focused

Lazarus et al (1984) theorized that during the appraisal phase of coping, individuals choose either an emotion-focused or problem-focused approach. The emotion-focused coping approach entails using primary appraisal techniques. Emotions are expressed and strategies such as perceiving the situation differently are used. The concern is with eliminating the emotional impact of the stressor. This is understandable as educational reform is here to stay, regardless of how teachers feel about it. In contrast, problem-focused approach entails using secondary appraisal techniques, and learning new ways to change the stressor. A problem-focused individual is more concerned with modifying or eradicating the source of stress. The goals of educational reform and means of achieving its objectives are clearly stated therefore it is unlikely that these will change because teachers view them as stressors. This strengthens the necessity to provide resources which will guide teachers in using effective coping strategies.

Several studies have documented the effectiveness and utilization of both emotion and problem-focused approaches when coping with stress. Bergin and Solman (1995) examined educational administrators' ability to cope during systematic restructuring in which the school system was being decentralized. Administrators who chose to use *emotion-focused strategies* responded by:

1. Redefining the problem
2. Increasing physical activities
3. Utilizing relaxation techniques to help deal with the negative feelings and emotions brought on during the reform.
4. Seeking emotional support while expressing emotions to other principals.

While some sought spiritual support, others sought to increase their alcohol consumption and smoked even more. Still others worried a lot, felt guilty, and procrastinated in making decisions.

Alternatively, 62% used a *problem-focused approach* in appraising and coping with stressors. As such, they engaged in:

1. Developing action plans
2. Gathering information
3. Developing problem solving approaches
4. Engaging in discussions of the issues while focusing on the positive aspects
5. Deriving specific goals and targets

6. Directing attention away from themselves and on to the requirements of the roles.

The latter is synonymous to a school that chooses to develop an action plan for raising student achievement, improving instructional approaches, and diverting attention from how they felt about the reform or poor assessment results.

In a study in which school administrators read coping statements and indicated to what extent each approach was effectively used in dealing with distressful occupational events or situations, Beuttner (1995) found that 66.7% of the principals self-rated their coping abilities as being highly effective. Problem solving emerged as the most used coping mechanism while escape-avoidance emerged as the least used, indicating that these principals used more of an analytical approach in dealing with the situation. Beuttner (1995) concluded that the results were largely based on principals' belief that their role is to solve conflict situations that arise in the educational organization. High scores indicated that seeking social support and practicing self-control were used and attributed to principals' need for support from colleagues, but at the same time maintaining the need to appear to be in control.

In a combined quantitative/qualitative research, Yiu-Chung, Kwok-Bun, Gina, and Kam-Weng (2000) found that teachers used varied approaches, emotion and problem-focused, when coping with stress. The most frequently used were:

1. Scrutinizing the problem and developing a direct-action approach

2. Changing perspectives by accepting the problem.
3. Relaxing
4. Suppressing anxious feelings
5. Seeking advice and support
6. Retreating from the problem
7. Seeking medical help
8. Drinking and smoking.

Interestingly, during the in-depth interview portion of the study, respondents indicated that seeking social support from school administrators was pointless, because administrators must follow directives handed down, and are powerless to make changes. This may very well be the case in some instances, as administrators are also held accountable for meeting demands. They are also affected by its impact, and as research indicate, are also experiencing stress in the form of *job-pressure, increased workload, and role overload*. In fairness however, teachers should still approach principals for support because more than likely they are utilizing coping strategies which teachers stand to benefit from, and at times strategies used at the building level can in fact make a difference. Yiu-Chung et al (2000) also noted that teachers' coping actions were manifested in task planning that would ultimately solve or modify problems. It was also concluded that teachers' coping action of changing perspectives is typical, especially in light of the realization that direct action without authority is pointless. It is a fact that implementing direct-action within the school depended on leverage from the school-building leadership. This conclusion was based on Swanson's (1989) explanation of cathartic expression in which individuals who were dealing with stressful situations realized that *life continues regardless*, therefore altering perspectives of stressors which stood no chance of changing, helped individuals in maintaining self–efficacy and acceptability.

> An individual's choice of coping mechanisms is not based on the type of stressor experienced; rather it is based on past experiences and peer influence (Yackel, 1983). According to Waters and Sroufe (1983), individuals possess and use a combination of internal and external stress-coping protectors, namely:

1. Social competence
2. Problem-solving ability
3. Mastery
4. Autonomy
5. Sense of purpose and future
6. Sense of agency or self-efficacy
7. Use of supportive groups.

Individuals are prone to use segments of each skill since flexibility in behavior is also deemed an important component in the selection of coping styles (Strelau, 1983). The fact that coping style greatly impacts and serves as an important variable in how individuals cope with stressful situations and events, makes sense, since many of the coping styles used in combating stress are packaged within stress management intervention programs, and are often rooted in techniques such as emotion-focused or problem-focused approaches (Roth, 1987; Walsh &

Vaughan, 1993; Lajoie & Shapiro, 1992; Benson, 1977; Ellis & Dryden, 1987; Pennebaker, 1997).

Coping: A Theoretical Examination of Techniques Used

An examination of each coping technique used will serve to help teachers in deciding which would be more beneficial as they seek to deal with stress emanating from high stakes demands. It also serves as a valuable insight for stress practitioners, policy makers, and educational leaders as they choose effective stress management intervention approaches.

Emotion-Focused:

Some of the most widely used emotion-focused techniques are *transcendental meditation, transpersonal meditation, relaxation, and exercise.* Roth (1987), operating from the premise that deep rest eliminates deep stress, describes transcendental meditation as a systematic technique in which the mind is fully awake yet calm and involved in a mental state of awareness. While transcendental meditation involves focusing quietly within, *transpersonal* extends the individual beyond himself; a process of moving humankind into functioning at the highest level of capability (Lajoie & Shapiro, 1992). Transpersonal meditation focuses on experiences in which individuals look beyond self for identity, and chooses instead to embrace a wider scope of humankind, psyche, and life (Walsh & Vaughan, 1993). Doing so involves individuals' understanding of a state of consciousness as part of the stress-relieving process. *Relaxation*

Response (Benson, 1977) is similar to transcendental experiences in that it allows you to sit quietly, relax, ignore distracting thoughts, and focus on positive situations encountered. This technique is practiced daily as a way of alleviating stressful feelings.

Problem-focused:

While some individuals may view emotion-focused strategies such as meditation and relaxation as passive approaches to alleviating stress, in contrast, problem-focused strategies are viewed as nudging participants to overt action. Rational-Emotive *Behavior* Therapy, an extension of Rational Emotive Therapy (Ellis, 1987) is one such strategy that forces stressed individuals to take responsibility for their feelings. Rational Emotive Therapy is based on a premise that it is through our thoughts and interpretation of a situation, that we trigger positive or negative emotions. This may hold implications for how teachers view high stakes accountability demands. It also addresses evaluative beliefs, belief patterns, and self-efficacy. One underlying premise of this technique is that sheer introspection is unproductive but changing the belief process is more productive. It does not negate the fact however that negative and uncomfortable situations arise; rather it implores individuals to understand that it is through their response to these situations that emotions become inflamed. Ellis and Dryden (1987) stipulates guiding principles in the use of *Rational Emotive Behavioral Therapy*: Individuals should take responsibilities for their own emotions and become aware that harmful emotions and dysfunctional behaviors are basis of irrational beliefs. They should also learn realistic views immediately making these views a part of their existence, while basking in a reality-based perspective. Given the constraints of bureaucratic and centralized systems in which policies and directives take a top down approach, a reality-based perspective is essential. Individuals in some organizations are not likely to have stressful situations readily change based on *their suggestions* to effect system-wide changes. In such cases, individuals must retreat to an emotion-focused approach to alleviate feelings and symptoms of stress, or continue on the path of rational beliefs.

Actual problem solving takes place in several ways: Transfer-of-training and writing

As individuals participate in stress management workshops, transfer of training (Goldstein, 1989) is another premise in which actual problem solving takes place as individuals learn stress reduction strategies, and are expected to practice and transfer these strategies to the stressful setting. It begins with examination of the situation, getting beyond the emotions, and ultimately helping the brain to digest the event. This can be acquired by *writing* about experiences and stressful events (Pennebaker, 1997). The basic underlying principle of this concept is that as individuals write, it clears the mind, helps the inquiry process, and forces the individual to focus on the situation in an analytical fashion. It is this prolonged focus that starts the problem-solving process because assessing and identifying stressors is the first step to assisting individuals to code or classify their experiences. For example, teachers may not understand why it is that they view instructional audits or public scrutiny of assessments results so negatively. Identification and classification of the factors leading up to these feelings, is the first step to dealing with the identified triggers.

SECTION FOUR

Stress Management Programs for Educators: A Necessity

Recognizing that stress is a variable that impacts many teachers during high stakes educational reform, policy makers, and educational leaders may wish to consider incorporating stress management as part of teacher-required professional development. To ignore teachers' need for stress reduction strategies is to disregard research detailing the obstruction to student achievement that results from teacher stress (Guglielmi & Tatrow, 1998). Taking into consideration the fact that stress bears physical ramifications (Seyle, 1984) supports the suggestion that intervention needs to be administered to offset physical outcomes of stress. McGrath's (1976) explanation of stress also supports the contention that as educators identify certain aspects of their job as being stressful, and perceive an imbalance between the demands placed on them and the ability to deal with the consequences set forth, they will experience a high level of stress; hence the need for availability of teachers' stress management programs specifically designed to incorporate effective coping strategies.

Stress Management Programs: Goals, Approaches, and Design

In the event school systems respond to the appeal for stress management intervention they may choose to incorporate it at the organizational level, or outsource the job to private businesses. In any event, educators must decide if all teachers will receive stress management training proactively as a part of professional development or reactively, after teachers have exhibited stress. *Stress Management for Teachers* would be ideal mainly because it would address stressors that impact teachers specifically. During an examination of businesses that offer stress management training, educators must be able to recognize design flaws, and assess the effectiveness of these programs by being cognizant of underlying theories upon which stress management programs are based. In the event colleges or school districts decide to create their own stress management programs, the first step is to identify the goals, and decide whether the programs should take a holistic, team-focused, or relational training approach. Simply providing employees with handouts, flyers, and pamphlets on the subject of stress, without actual stress management training is insufficient. Nonetheless, using these as supplemental resources in addition to training is ideal.

Stress Management Interventions: Three Levels

Stress management intervention can be offered at one of three levels: primary, secondary, and tertiary. (Dewe, 1994). The decision to offer stress management training/intervention at a primary, secondary, or tertiary level is based on the organization's objectives and perspectives. If an *environment-based perspective* is taken to stress management training, focus will be on making changes in job design, work setting, work situations, and performance appraisal feedback (Rees & Redfern, 2000). This perspective bears implication for school administrators who are responsible for curriculum, scheduling, staffing, and workload. Focusing on job redesign and controlling workload is considered intervening at a primary level. In contrast, if a *person-based perspective* is chosen, the program will take a secondary approach to stress management in which focus is placed on helping individuals learn to cope with stress (Rees et al, 2000). In so doing, teachers would learn how to take flexible approaches to their jobs, develop a readiness to accept and use feedback, and most of all develop a willingness to take on additional tasks. Imagine a school in which teachers are adaptable, share ideas and utilize feedback, and are willing to rise to the occasion. A school in which teachers are motivated to go beyond what is required so that the school meets accountability demands.

Rees et al encourages the use of both perspectives when designing stress management programs. It is unfortunate that some organizations neglect to deal with stress at a primary or secondary level, choosing rather to do so at a tertiary level by providing only rehabilitative stress management through Employees Assistance Programs. An organization's dedication to eliminating or reducing work-related stress, is reflected in the level at which its interventions are designed. Once a school system decides at what level stress management training/intervention will be offered, the next step is to consider two factors; the benefit of including educational leaders in training, and research-based recommendations for programs design.

Leadership-Participation:

A major criticism of stress management programs is the absence of organizational leaders. It is imperative that organizational leaders know how to *identify signs of stress*. Without this knowledge, leaders will be unable to signify a need for employee assistance when it is most needed. This inaction ultimately puts an organization and its employees at risk (Dewe & O'Driscoll, 1992; Adams, 1989). In a study of 540 managers, conducted to determine leaders' views on stress and beliefs about stress management programs (Dewe & O'Driscoll, 2002) only 48% of the managers were capable of identifying signs of stress. When asked whose responsibility it would be to initiate stress management, only 22.9% believed that the organization should provide special assistance through employee assistance programs, while 22% believed that it was the employee's responsibility to locate stress management assistance. Such findings are among the reasons attributed to stress management programs' failures. When leaders have this mindset it serves as a prelude to tertiary level interventions; a reactive approach in which help is offered at a late stage. Leaders who are capable of identifying the signs of stress, and who care enough to have the organization take responsibility for intervention measures, will choose a proactive approach.

Stress Management Program Design: *Concerns and Focus*

Along with recommendations for appropriately planning and designing stress management programs, researchers have also ventured to criticize designs deemed as flawed. Dewe (1994) asserts that the development of stress management programs in organizations have been affected by power, ethics and control. Further, programs have quite often been rejected by organizations as it became evident that structural changes would be necessary as part of the stress reducing intervention. In such cases, organizations resort to dealing with stress by treating the symptom and not the cause. It is heartening to know however that educational leaders have flexibility in work design at the building level (environment-based perspective).

Huberman and Vandenberghe (1999) advise that stress management programs should address two challenges:
1) A guarantee that planned changes embody the generic elements of stress
2) A representation of these elements within the intervention environment. Conducting these programs within the actual school

setting would allow a representation of the elements that are within the school and are deemed to be stressors. It means then that stress practitioners would be able to model responses and coping strategies directly.

To minimize the chance of designing stress management programs that are insufficiently theory-based (Murphy, 1995) and narrowly focused, an examination of the underlying theories upon which each program is designed should be conducted. In addition, a comprehensive approach targeting both individuals and the organization, and one in which employees participate in planning and design is necessary to avoid designing a program that is narrowly focused. Properly identifying and assessing the need for intervention is a necessary precursor to designing *effective* stress management programs (Wallerstein & Weinger, 1992) because if needs are not properly identified then the objective being aspired to may be incorrect.

Evaluation of Stress Management Programs

Armed with the knowledge that stress management programs should be theory based, and reflective of clear and specific goals, a journey into empirical and non-empirical findings of stress management programs being used in the field is necessary. In so doing, several designs, approaches, and underlying theories will be noted. These designs consists of Spark's (1983) holistic approach, Hearn's (2001) coaching; Slavin's (1996) therapeutic group involvement; Jesus and Conboy's (2001) relational training approach; and Sokol and Aiello's (1993) onsite team-focused approach. As each approach is examined, it is important to note a common concern: *intervention effect over time.* Realistically speaking, as school systems consider providing stress management training for teachers, budget allocations will become a major focus therefore programs with tremendous *intervention effect over time* will factor into cost effectiveness.

Holistic Design:

Sparks (1983) cautions that unless a holistic approach is employed in stress management program design, the effect of each program will be short-lived. A holistic approach in which active-problem solving is used to address stress, from a physical and psychological standpoint, is deemed to be effective in tackling four major goals:

1) Reducing isolation
2) Restoring perspective and balance
3) Increasing self-awareness
4) Identifying the next step.

Sparks (1983) asserts that the objective of *reducing isolation* is to reduce the physical remoteness in which teachers work, and bring them together for sharing, strategizing, and brainstorming. It is contended that as teachers are isolated from each other they are unable to capitalize on the rewards that sharing information with each other can bring. *Restoration of perspective* and balance is believed to happen as teachers regain focus through sharing, and remembering the accomplishment and satisfactions achieved from teaching rather than continuously dwell on negative situations encountered on the job. *Increasing awareness* is achieved as teachers learn to recognize when they are stressed, and identify the source of their stressors. This must be followed by stress-reducing strategies on a continuous basis. Supporting theory for the development of holistic stress management programs is congruent with Pearlin and Schooler's (1978) assertion that stress management activities should consists of three categories:

1) Techniques for controlling the physical and psychological consequences of stress;

2) Thought modification techniques for changing the perspective and meaning of a stressful situation.

3) Using professional support groups and organizational change strategies to effect a change.

The *Consortium for Research on Emotional Intelligence in Organization* reported the successful and effective use of holistic stress management training in a major organization, Corning, INC. In collaboration with Jeff Murphy of the National Institute for Occupational Safety and Health (NIOSH), and Jeff Monroy, Hank Jonas, and Joseph Mathey of Corning, INC, the holistic stress management program design incorporated the four goals Sparks (1983) alluded to. Isolation was reduced by conducting stress management training in groups where participants, including managers, were able to listen to speakers share their experiences and include them in stress reducing activities. As participants focused on various stress reducing strategies, they were assured that these strategies were uncomplicated and may at some point have been used by each person, but not unwaveringly. This broke down the barriers allowing participants to feel comfortable in sharing and experimenting with the strategies.

Tapes on guided imagery were given to each participant with the hope of encouraging the use of skills learned outside of the setting. Besides, the physical aspect of holistic training was not forgotten as participants were given the opportunity to, at their convenience, participate in yoga, tai chi, and massage. In keeping with the tenets of holistic training, participants were also required to practice stress-reducing strategies on a daily basis, and return to class with their questions. Support group lists were established, giving them an opportunity to create dyads, calling each other with questions at any time between sessions. Additionally, formative assessments were used at the end of the first, eighth, and twelve-week periods to determine participants' stress level, awareness of stress, and use of stress-reducing strategies. Results indicated that significant changes occurred in participants' stress symptoms and ability to cope.

On-site Team-focused Design

Sokol and Aiello (1993) experimented with an onsite team-focused approach. This was based on Goldstein's (1989) theory of *transfer-of-*

training and essential conditions for effective transfer. Essential conditions in place were:

1) Dramatizations of materials and strategies
2) Examples of stressful situations encountered on the job
3) Full employee participation
4) Job site venues for training.

Prior to starting, each participant completed a self-report questionnaire in which they identified perceived work related stressors. Four intact-teams, along with managers and supervisors, attended two half-day training sessions. The first day's focus was stress awareness, and the second was stress management practice.

First training day included employees' participation in the following:

1) Review of participation guidelines
2) Defining stress
3) Identifying stress symptoms within themselves and others
4) Targeting sources of stress
5) Using behavioral and cognitive activities along with self-talk to reduce tension and increase awareness
6) Learning stress management strategies through scenario writing and problem solving techniques
7) Through the use of diaries and discussions learn how to monitor stress.

On the second day, participants practiced stress management through:

1) Discussion

2) Exercises

3) Perspective building

4) Active listening

5) Structured coaching

6) Positive self-talk

7) Cognitive reframing.

8) Managing time-related stress.

During training, participants formed groups, discussed coworkers' and customers' signs of stress, and shared stressful experiences while brainstorming effective strategies for managing stress. Discussions regarding time-management focused on how the actions of all co-workers impacted on everyone. **Note:** *Participants became aware that excessive absenteeism created an undulating effect and incited stressful situations, thereby increasing other coworkers' workload.* Astoundingly, managers and supervisors abandoned their supervisory roles and chose to function as peers while participating in group discussions and activities.

Upon completion of the workshops, several follow-ups were used to determine the extent to which transfer-of-training took place. *Four weeks after training,* managers and supervisors interviewed participants regarding the value and impact of the stress management-training program. Participants expressed thanks for the opportunity to develop the ability to recognize stress in themselves and others. They desired additional workshops, requested copies of relaxation videos, and showered praise for the practical strategies offered in the stress management program. Through a *two-month follow-up* survey, employees expressed success in being able to recognize self-induced stress, co-workers' stress, and time-related and customers' stress.

Managers indicated that they were successful in being able to identify customer and co-worker stress, and liked the fact that employees had begun joking about stress. While Sokol et al. (1993) recognized that participants had successfully mastered the ability to recognize and acknowledge stress; they were disappointed in the low level of transfer of training skills experienced by individuals, and concluded that the formation of dyads and triads would have served as support teams *after* stress management training. This supports the theory that transfer of training is more effective at a group level rather than on an individual level.

Coaching:

While Sokol et al promotes an onsite team-focused approach, Hearn (2001) views one-on-one coaching as having a role in stress management. It is touted as being extremely beneficial considering that it deals with the entire person on an individual basis, and takes an action-based problem solving approach. Coaching is also positively viewed because it determines where the person is in terms of stress, provides greater focus and awareness, and helps in defining what clients want. Hearn (2001) also addressed transfer-of-training by theorizing that transfer of learning is better served through coaching because while stress management trainers leave, coaches remain with individuals consistently through the stress relieving process. Regardless of what stress management program is selected, teachers must be able to recognize when they are experiencing distress, and likewise administrators should be able to identify, recommend, and encourage stressed teachers to see a coach.

Hearn considered coaching to be extremely effective in several instances, namely:

1.) When clients experienced stress as a result of working with difficult team-members they often found themselves coping by *avoiding* those members. Avoidance as a coping technique was impractical in a team environment therefore appropriate and effective stress management techniques were sought. For these clients, coaching taught them how to transfer focus from themselves onto disruptive team members. *Through coaching*, clients learned the following:

- Behavior modification to increase self-confidence.
- How to properly assess the situation, realizing that the problem was only being appraised as distressful due to a lack of self-confidence and need to be valued.
- How to reduce the need to be valued so that no longer would negative tones and insinuations from disruptive employees be viewed as stressors.
- Strategies involved in developing an action plan.

2) Clients whose stress was workload-related benefited from coaching by:
- Learning how to slow down and regroup.
- Changing beliefs and perspectives.
- Quietening the mind daily through relaxation techniques.
- Practicing self-control through relaxation.

3) Clients whose stress was based on pressure of decision-making, benefited from coaching by:
- Learning to consider values and vision before making decisions.
- Practicing daily writing to identify issues before they became stressors.
- Practicing taking long deep breaths before giving responses.

Comprehensive School-wide Health Program Design

Massey (1998) takes a different view regarding how stress management in school systems should be handled and argues that in light of stress research findings, schools should handle stress management through a comprehensive school health program. This assertion was based on Allenworth, Lawson, Nicholson, and Wyche's (1997) comprehensive model, which consisted of four elements:

1) Community participation and focus
2) School environment

3) Education

4) Services.

Implementation of this model would entail involving the community and parents in stress management by communicating the value of wellness programs. This can be done through newsletters, family health night, health fairs, and guest speakers. The underlying supporting theory of this model is Pransky's (1991) theory that school health programs decreased absenteeism and increased teacher morale. Massey (1991) further emphasize that stress management can be infused in most areas of the curriculum through: creative and expressive writing in language arts classes, meditation and yoga as part of various cultures in social studies, discussion of physiological and psychological stress responses in science classes, and expressions of thoughts in art classes with the benefits being evident in psychologically healthy staff and students.

Therapeutic Group Involvement Approach:

Slavin (1996) takes a therapeutic-group approach to handling stress in an educational environment hypothesizing that if teachers are able to process their needs through therapeutic group involvement, they would be more likely to use opportunities for selfless and constructive fulfillment, hence benefiting their students. The underlying theory of this approach is based on Peck and Mitchell's (1962) theory that the teaching profession is largely based on need fulfillment, and the belief that teacher stress stems from:

1. Repression and distortion of their feelings.

Understanding Teacher Stress

2. A sense of being misunderstood and ignored by school administrators.
3. Feelings of inadequacy, believing that they occupy only a small space in a large organization.
4. Internal emotional pressures based on their mental and physiological well being.
5. Isolation from adult colleagues.

In a five-year study, Slavin (1996) examined the effect of group therapy on teacher stress in a New York school setting. With the principal's approval, school stationary was used to communicate information about the group's existence, venue, and meeting time. During the first meeting, a group contract concerning voluntary participation, confidentiality, meeting time, and group notes, was read and signed. Teachers were aware that they could withdraw at anytime, and that individual disclosures should not be discussed outside of the group. Late arrivals and early departures were also acceptable. Several adjustments had to be made in order to gain teachers' trust. The name *therapy* was dropped to avoid stigma, and teachers were assured that anything discussed would not be shared with administration. Once all these were in place, teachers began freely expressing themselves.

The first year entailed building trust and sharing experiences. It was noted that as teachers shared experiences they became more relaxed. The second year's focus was creating and maintaining group harmony, which was achieved as members became supportive and protective, cushioning each other in stressful times. By the third year, participants were able to tolerate differences in opinions and reactions. Everyone began taking responsibility for their own behavior, while empathizing with each other. Self-confidence increased and unresolved conflicts were brought out in the open and dealt with. The fourth year saw an increase in participants, as colleagues saw how mentally healthy and less stressed group members were. The fifth year became temporarily unstable as five of the initial group members transferred to other schools. Group members were deeply saddened by the loss.

An evaluation of the five-year study showed that the objective was met. An emotionally safe climate was developed, allowing teachers a place to explore and understand their feelings and reactions to various stressors. Teachers supported each other, and were able to understand how stressful situations impacted their students and colleagues. As such, they became more empathetic and tolerant.

Relational Training Approach:

Jesus and Conboy's (2001) relational training approach to stress management is rooted in Rational Emotive Therapy (Ellis & Dryden, 1987), which seeks to replace an individual's irrational beliefs, a belief that there is a relationship between emotions and behavior and that motivation is based on a belief in the ability to execute the necessary behavior (Bandura, 1977). In application, *it implies that motivated teachers are more apt to promote educational reform because they believe that they possess the ability to implement the objectives set forth by reform policies*. During a 30-hour stress management program, relational-training approach incorporating direct and active participation in a supportive environment was disseminated through *ten sessions*. Each session addressed a particular component.

Session One: Self-report instruments were administered to measure participant's level of stress, subjective perception of well being, irrational beliefs. Participants also reviewed the stress management program, and took part in relaxation exercise in a positive relational climate.

Session Two: Participants defined and identified stressors in addition to assessing appraisals that often led to feelings of inefficacy and professional incompetence.

Session Three: Participants discussed possible coping strategies, and developed individual coping plans.

Session Four: Rational-Emotive Therapy (Ellis, 1987) was used to assess irrational beliefs and eliminate or change irrational thoughts. This process entailed convincing participants that the source of stress was within *their belief pattern*, and *not* the actual event. Participants learned belief-changing strategies that would move them from a rigid and irrational belief style of thinking onto a more rational belief system.

Session Five: Participants explored cognitive and physical controlling techniques such as breathing exercises, muscular relaxation, voice placing, and relaxation by imagination.

Session Six: Team management strategies were taught to combat noted feelings of isolation, and teamwork strategies were used to cope with increased workload.

Session Seven: Role-playing was used as participants practiced verbal and non-verbal assertiveness and communication skills.

Session Eight: Effective strategies for improving classroom relationships and students' motivation to reach their goals were learned and practiced.

Session Nine: The focus was on participants helping each other with managing classroom disruption. Teamwork and exchange of professional experiences were both used to accomplish this task.

Session Ten: Subjective analyses. The final session was used to recap many of the exercises practiced, techniques demonstrated and discussed, and finally to assess the effectiveness of the stress training program.

A post-test was administered to determine the effect of relational training and results indicated a significant reduction in stress and irrational beliefs, and significant increase in professional motivation and perception of well-being. Results of the subjective analyses during the final session, served to influence an extension of the course from 30 to 50 hours. Teachers unanimously indicated that the course needed to be longer in duration to make time for deeper analyses. The extension granted more time for practicing teamwork and assertiveness training, and for adding healthy lifestyles training to the program.

Conclusion

As educators we bear a tremendous responsibility for student-performance. It is the nature of our job, and is indeed a tall order. Our classrooms reflect a mosaic of differences and issues to which we must respond even before we are able to teach. We gladly respond to our students' physical, emotional, and psychological needs and are constantly aware that on any given day, we spend the greatest portion of their waking moments educating them. This we take seriously. We bask in the knowledge that our students' values are influenced by what we do, therefore we give of ourselves unfailingly. It is virtually impossible to calculate the true cost of our giving as we work tirelessly throughout many nights grading papers and selflessly spending numerous weekends preparing demonstrations and planning lessons to guide our students in concept and skill formation. We cringe at criticism of our efforts when our students do not perform as well as is expected but we never shirk our responsibilities. We can be seen returning each year with vigilance, ready to try new theories and strategies. Ready once again to make it work. Teachers are indeed a tenacious and resilient people. With all our giving and tireless pursuit, we need to replenish that great reservoir of intestinal fortitude. In so doing, we seek to develop an awareness of avenues and outlets available for replenishment? An awareness that self-care is important is the driving force behind our determination to reduce isolation, and increase dialogue and personal support among colleagues. Supplies and support are what we need most. We are aware that as our education system participates in continuous improvement, no doubt accountability demands will increase. The knowledge that consequences are associated therewith is not comforting, nonetheless, our determination to forge ahead continues……

REFERENCES

Adams, J. D. (1989). *Understanding and managing stress: Instruments to assess your lifestyle.* San Diego, California: University Associates.

Allenworth, D. D., Lawson, E., Nicholson, Lois., & Wyche, J. (1997). *Schools and Health: Our Nation's Investment.* Washington, DC: National Academy Press.

Allinder, R. M. (1994). The relationship between efficacy and the instructional practices of special education teachers and consultants. *Teacher Education and Special Education, 17,* 86-95.

Armenakis, A. A., Harris, S. G., & Mossholder, K. (1993). Creating readiness for organizational change . Human Relations, 46, 1-23

Bandura, A. (1988). Self-efficacy conception of anxiety. *Anxiety Research, An International Journal, 1,* 77-98.

Bandura, A. (1997). *Self-efficacy: The exercise of control.* New York: Freeman

Beatty R. W., & Ulrich D. (1991). Re-energizing the Mature Organization. *Organizational Dynamics,* 20, 16–30.

Beuttner, R. P. (1995). Coping mechanisms used by rural principals in Saskatchewan in response to stressful events. Unpublished master's thesis, University of Regina, Saskatchewan, Canada.

Bergin, M., & Solman, R. (1995). Coping with restructuring: A study of senior educational administrators. *Journal of Educational Administration, 33* (2), 52.

Benson, H. (1977). *The Relaxation Response.* New York: William Morrow and Company, Inc., p.114.

Boyer, E. L. (1988). Report card on school reform. Princeton, NJ: Carnegie Foundation for the Advancement of Teaching.

Bruno, J. E. (2002). The geographical distribution of teacher absenteeism in large urban school district settings: Implications for school reform efforts aimed at promoting equity and excellence in education. *Education Policy Analysis Archives, 10 (32).* Retrieved December 12, 2003 from http://eppa.asu.edu/epaa/v10321.

Campbell, J. P. (1990). Modeling the performance predictive problem in Industrial and Organizational psychology. In M. D. Dunnette & L. M. Houghs (Eds.), Handbook of Industrial and Organizational Psychology (2nd ed.) vol 1, pp. 687-732. Palo Alto, CA: Consulting Psychologist Press.

Cencirulo, R. S. (2001). *The relationship between hardiness and job satisfaction in elementary school teachers.* (Doctoral dissertation, La Sierra University, 2001). Dissertation Abstract International, 62, 1279.

Chance, E. W. (1992). Visionary leadership in schools: Successful strategies for developing and implementing an educational vision. Springfield, IL.

Cooley, V. E., & Shen, J. (2003). School accountability and professional job responsibilities: A perspective from secondary principals. *NASSP Bulletin, 87*(634), 10-25.

Cox, H., & Wood, J. R. (1980). Organizational structure and professional alienation: The case of public school teachers. *Peabody Journal of Education,* 58(1).

Cusick, P. A. (2003). A study of Michigan's school principal shortage. Policy Report No. 12. Education Policy Center: Michigan State University.

Dewe, P. J. (1994). EAPs and stress management from theory to practice to comprehensiveness. Personnel Review, 23, 21-32.

Dewe, P., & O'Driscoll, M.P. (2002). Stress management interventions: What do managers actually do? *Personnel Review, 31*(2), 143-165.

Dunham, J. (1992). Stress in teaching (2nd. Ed.). New York: Routledge.

Ealy, G. M. E. (1993). The relationship between anxiety and self-efficacy of urban elementary school teachers (Urban Teachers). (Doctoral dissertation, Wayne State University, 1993). Dissertation Abstract International, 55, 0190.

Ellis, A. (1987). Integrative developments in rational-emotive therapy (RET). *Journal of Integrative and Eclectic Psychotherapy, 6,* 470-479.

Ellis, A., & Dryden, W. (1987). *The Practice of Rational-Emotional Therapy.* New York: Springer.

Freeman, S. J. & Cameron, K. S. (1993). Organizational downsizing: A convergence and reorientation framework. Organization science, 4(1), 10, 29.

Flynn, P. (2000). Identification of the level and perceived causes of stress and burnout among high school principals in South Carolina. (Doctoral dissertation, University of South Carolina, 2000). Dissertation Abstracts International, 61, 2532.

Garrity, M. L. (2001). *Teacher retirement: A study of the conditions affecting teachers' retirement decisions in Massachuse*tts. (Doctoral dissertation, University of Massachusetts, 2001), Dissertation Abstracts International, 62, 405.

Goldstein, I. L. (1989). *Training and Development in Organizations, 3rd Edition.* San Francisco: Jossey Bass Publishing.

Gordon, L. M. (2001, Spring). High teacher efficacy as a marker of teacher effectiveness in the domain of classroom management. Paper presented at the annual meeting of the California council on teacher education. San Diego, California.

Greenwood, G. E., Olejnik, S. F., & Parkay, F. W. (1990). Relationships between four teacher efficacy belief patterns and selected teacher characteristics. *Journal of Research and Development in Education, 23*(2), 102-106.

Guglielmi, SA. R., & Tatrow, K. (1998). Occupational stress, burnout, and health in teachers: A methodological and theoretical analysis. *Review of educational research.* 68, (1), 61-91.

Hanisch, K. A. (2000). The impact of organizational interventions on behaviors: An examination of different models of withdrawal. In D. R. Ilgen & C. L. Hulin (Eds.), *Computational modeling of behavior in organizations: The third scientific discipline* (pp. 33-60). Washington, DC: American Psychological Association.

Hearn, W. (2001). The role of coaching in stress management. *Stress News, 13* (2).

Heiser, L. A. (2001). The impact of teacher termination on the level of stress of elementary principals. (Doctoral dissertation, Lynn University, 2001). Dissertation Abstract International, 62, 3254.

Howley, A., & Pendarvis, E. (2002). Recruiting and retaining rural school administrators (ERIC Digest No. EDO-RC-02-7). Charleston, WV: ERIC Clearinghouse on Rural Education and Small Schools. (ERIC Document Reproduction Service No. Pending).

Huberman, A. M., & Vandenberghe, R. (1999). Introduction -- burnout and the teaching profession. In R. Vandenberghe, & Huberman, A. M. (Ed.), *Understanding and preventing teacher burnout: A sourcebook of international research and practice* (pp. 1-12). Cambridge: Cambridge University Press.

Jesus, S. N. de. & Conboy, J. (2001). A stress management course to prevent teacher distress. *The International Journal of Educational Management, 15* (3).

Kahn, R. L., Wolfe, D. M., Quinn, R. P., Snoek, J. D. & Rosenthal, R. A, (1964). *Organizational stress: Studies in role conflict and ambiguity.* New York, NY: John Wiley and Sons.

Kobasa, S. C., & Puccetti, M. (1983). Personality and social resources in stress resistance. *Journal of Personality and Social Psychology 45,* 839-850.

Kyriacou, C., & Sutcliffe, J. (1978). A model of teacher stress. *Educational Studies, 4,* 1-6.

Kyriacou, C. (1987). Teacher stress and burnout: An international review. *Educational Research, 29,* 146-152.

Lajoie, D. H. & Shapiro, S. I. (1992). Definitions of transpersonal psychology: The first twenty-three years. *Journal of Transpersonal Psychology, 24,* 91.

Lazarus, R. S., & Folkman, S. (1984). *Stress, appraisal, and coping.* New York: Springer.

Leanna, C. R., & Barry, B. (2000). Stability and change as simultaneous experiences in organizational life. *Academy of Management Review, 25*(4), 753-759.

Lim, V. C. (1997). Moderating effects of work-based support on the relationship between job insecurity and its consequences. *Work and Stress, 11,* 251-266

Maddi, S. R. (2002). The story of hardiness: Twenty years of theorizing, research, and practice, Consulting Psychology Journal: Practice and Research, 54, 173-184.

Massey, M. S. (1998). The role of comprehensive school health programs. Washington, DC: ERIC Clearinghouse on Teaching and Teacher Education.

Maturi, R. (1992, July 20). Stress can be beaten. *Industry Week,* 24(14), 22-25.

McGrath, J. E. (1976). Stress and behavior in organizations. In, M. D. Dunnette (Ed.), *Handbook of Industrial and organizational Psychology* (pp. 1351-1395). Chicago: Rand McNally College Publishing.

Moriarity, V., Edmonds, S., Blatchford, P., & Martin, C. (2001). Teaching young children: Perceived satisfaction and stress. *Educational Research, 43*(1), 33-47.

Murphy, R. L. (1995). Managing stress. *Personnel Review, 24,* 41-50.

Nelson, A., Cooper, C. L., & Jackson, P. (1995). Uncertainty amidst change: The impact of privatization on employees' job satisfaction and well being. *Journal of Occupational and Organizational Psychology, 68,* 57-71.

Ones, D. S. (2002). Introduction to special issue on counterproductive behaviors at work. *International journal of selection and assessment, 10,* 1-4.

Pearlin, L. I & Schooler, C. (1978). The structure of coping. *Journal of Health and Social Behavior, 19,* 2-21. Peck, R. E., & Mitchell, J. V. (1962). *Mental Health.* Washington, DC: National Educational Association.

Peck, R. E., & Mitchell, Jr., J.V. (1962). *Mental Health.* Washington, D.C.: National Educational Association.

Pennebaker, J.W. (1997). *Opening Up: The Healing Power of Expressing Emotions (Revised).* New York: Guilford Press.

Porter, L., Steers, R., Mowday, R., & Boulian, P. (1974). Organizational commitment, job satisfaction, and turnover among psychiatric technicians. *Journal of Applied Psychology, 59,* 603-609.

Possner, I., & Leitner, A. L (1981). Eustress versus distress: Determination by predictability and controllability of the stressor. Stress: *The Official Journal of the International Institute of Stress and its Affiliates*, summer 1981.

Pransky, J. (1991). *Prevention: The critical need.* Springfield, MO: Burrel Foundation & Paradigm Press.

Rees, C., & Redfern, D. (2000). Recognizing the perceived causes of stress - a training and development perspective. *Industrial and Commercial Training. 32* (4). 120-127.

Romanelli, E. & Tushman, M. L. (1994). Organizational transformation as punctuated equilibrium: An empirical test. *Academy of Management Journal, 37,* 1141-1166.

Ross, J. A. (1992). Teacher efficacy and the effect of coaching on student achievement. Canadian Journal of Education, 17 (1), 51-65.

Roth, R. (1987). *Transcendental Meditation.* Iowa: Maharishi Intl University of Management

Ryan, T. (2001). A comparison of the reported stress level of Massachusetts secondary schools principals and their schools' scores on the 1999 MCAS. (Doctoral dissertation, Seton Hall University, 2001). Dissertation Abstracts International, 62, 44.

Schulte, D. P. (2000). A test driven accountability system in Texas: Principals' voices. (Doctoral dissertation, University of Texas at El Paso, 2000) Dissertation Abstracts International, 61. 4355.

Seaward, B. L. (1997). *Managing stress: Principles and strategies for health and well being (2nd Ed).* Boston, Mass: Jones and Bartlett.

Seyle, H., (1975), Homeostasis and the reactions to stress: A discussion of Walter B. Cannon's contributions. *In The Life and Contributions of Walter Bradford Cannon 1871-1945.* New York: State University of New York, Downstate Medical Centre.

Slack-Williams, D. (1996). The relationship of self-efficacy and state-trait anxiety with the coping abilities of secondary teachers: Regular and special education. Unpublished doctoral dissertation. Wayne State University.

Slavin, R. L. (1996). An onsite stress workshop for teachers: The creation of a therapeutic Group involvement. *Group, 20* (2), 131-144.

Sokol, M. B., & Aiello, J. R. (1993). Implications for team focused stress management training. Consulting Psychology Journal. 45.(4). 1-10.

Sparks. D. (1983). Practical solutions for teacher stress. *Theory into practice, 22*(1), 33-42.

Spitulnik, N. R. (2001). How elementary principals perceive the changes in their roles and their schools as a result of Massachusetts education reform. (Doctoral dissertation, University of Massachusetts Amherst, 2001). .Dissertation Abstract International, 62, 45.

Stein, M. K., Wang, M. C. (1988). Teacher development and school improvement: The process of teacher change. Teaching and Teacher Education, 4, 171-187.

Strelau. J. (1983). *Temperament, personality, activity.* London: Academic

Swanson, G. (1989). On the motives and motivation of selves. In D. D, Frank., & E. D. McCarthy. The Sociology of Emotion: Original Essays and Research Papers. Greenwich, Connecticut: JAI Press.

Turchi, L., Johnson, D., Owens, D. D., & Montgomery, D. (2002). Paper presented at the Annual Meeting of the American Educational Research Association (April 2002).

Van Sell, M., Brief, A., Schuler, R. (1977). Role conflict and role ambiguity: A review and synthesis of the literature. Working paper 76-30A. University of Iowa, Iowa City.

Wallerstein and Weinger, 1992

Walsh, R. & Vaughan, F. (Eds.). (1993). *Paths beyond ego: The transpersonal vision* (p. 3). Los Angeles, CA: J. P. Tarcher.

Waters, E. and Sroufe, L. (1983). Social Competence as a Developmental Construct. *Developmental Review, 3,* 79-97.

Woolfolk, R. I., & Richardson, F. C. (1978). *Stress, Sanity, and Survival.* New York: New American Library.

Yackel, I. (1983). An analysis of leadership styles and stresses in the rural principalship. Unpublished master's thesis, University of Regina, SK.

Yiu-Chung Ko., Kwok-Bun Chan., Gina Lai., & Kam-Weng Boey. (2000). Stress and Coping of Singapore Teachers: A Quantitative and Qualitative Analysis Journal of Developing Societies. Journal of Developing Societies, 16. (2).

About The Author

Dr. Andrea Thompson, member of the National Sorority of Phi Delta Kappa, Inc. currently works with one of Maryland's largest school districts, Prince Georges County. She also works with the Teacher Education Institute, Winter Park, Florida as an Online/Distance Education Instructor where she guides teachers in effectively integrating technology. Dr. Thompson received a B.Sc. degree in Industrial Arts Education from University of Maryland Eastern Shore, M.Sc. degree in Educational Media from Nova Southeastern University, and a Ph.D. in Leadership and Administration from Barry University in Florida. She currently resides in Silver Spring, Maryland with her husband and four children.

Printed in the United States
45549LVS00004B/13-111